# GEORGE WASHINGTON

## FATHER OF THE NATION

TRACIE EGAN

rosen central
**Primary Source**™

The Rosen Publishing Group, Inc., New York

Published in 2004 by The Rosen Publishing Group, Inc.
29 East 21st Street, New York, NY 10010

### Library of Congress Cataloging-in-Publication Data

Egan, Tracie.
George Washington / Tracie Egan.— 1st ed.
  p. cm. — (Primary sources of famous people in American History)
Summary: A biography of the commander in chief of the Continental army and first president of the United States, George Washington.
Includes bibliographical references and index.
ISBN 0-8239-4111-6 (lib. bdg.)
ISBN 0-8239-4183-3 (pbk. bdg.)
6-pack ISBN 0-8239-4310-0
1. Washington, George, 1732–1799—Juvenile literature. 2. Presidents—United States—Biography—Juvenile literature. 3. Generals—United States—Biography—Juvenile literature. [1. Washington, George, 1732–1799. 2. Presidents.]
I. Title. II. Series: Primary sources of famous people in American History (New York, N.Y.)
E312.66 .E35 2003
973.4'1'092—dc21

2002152423

*Manufactured in the United States of America*

**Photo credits:** cover © Bequest of Mrs. Benjamin Ogle Tayloe, Collection of the Corcoran Gallery of Art/Corbis; pp. 5 (top), 18 Library of Congress Geography and Map Division; p. 5 (bottom) National Portrait Gallery, Smithsonian Institution/Art Resource, NY; pp. 6, 7 (bottom), 29 courtesy of the Mt. Vernon Ladies' Association; pp. 7 (top), 21, 23 (bottom), 24 Library of Congress Manuscript Division; p. 9 (top) Edward Savage, *The Washington Family*, Andrew W. Mellon Collection, photo © 2003 Board of Trustees, National Gallery of Art, Washington; p. 9 (bottom) Robert Creamer and the Dr. Samuel D. Harris National Museum of Dentistry; pp. 10, 19 © Bettmann/Corbis; p. 11 Washington-Curtis-Lee Collection, Washington and Lee University, Lexington, VA; p. 13 © Hulton/Archive/Getty Images; pp. 14, 23 (top) Library of Congress Prints and Photographs Division; p. 15 The Phelps Stokes Collection, Miriam and Ira D. Wallach Division of Art, Prints and Photographs, The New York Public Library, Astor, Lenox, and Tilden Foundations; p. 16 courtesy of the George C. Neumann Collection, Valley Forge National Historic Park, photo by Cindy Reiman; p. 17 National Center for the American Revolution/The Valley Forge Historical Society; p. 20 Picture Collection, The Branch Libraries, New York Public Library, Astor, Lenox, and Tilden Foundations; p. 25 Art Resource, NY; p. 27 George Washington Papers, Manuscripts and Archives Division, The New York Public Library, Astor, Lenox, and Tilden Foundations; p. 28 © Kevin Fleming/Corbis.

Designer: Thomas Forget; Photo Researcher: Peter Tomlinson

# CONTENTS

# 1 THE FRENCH AND INDIAN WAR

George Washington led Americans to independence from England in the Revolutionary War. He then became the first president of the United States. Americans think of him as the father of their country.

## A COLONIAL OFFICER

After fighting in the French and Indian War, Washington retired from the British army in 1758. It was as a soldier for the British that he learned military tactics and the skills of leadership.

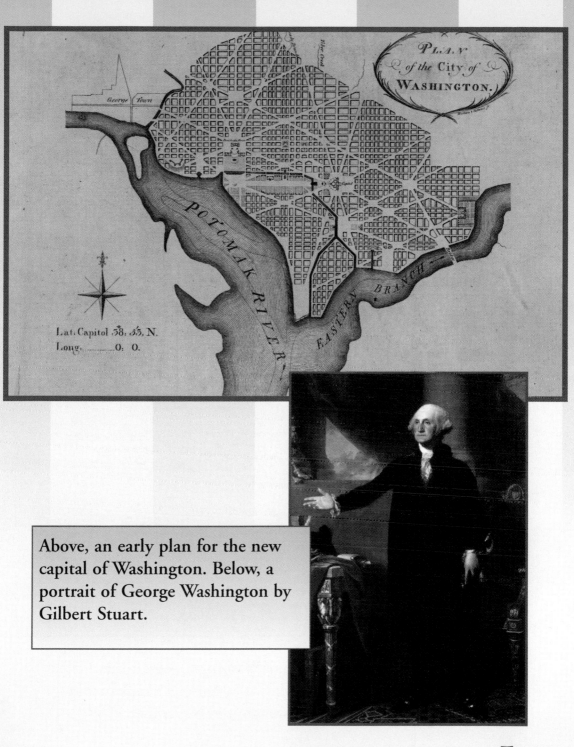

Above, an early plan for the new capital of Washington. Below, a portrait of George Washington by Gilbert Stuart.

In 1748, when Washington was 16 years old, he began working as a surveyor. Surveyors make maps and charts of unsettled land. George gained experience as a woodsman on his surveying trips.

When his older half-brother, Lawrence, died, George inherited his plantation in Virginia. It was called Mount Vernon.

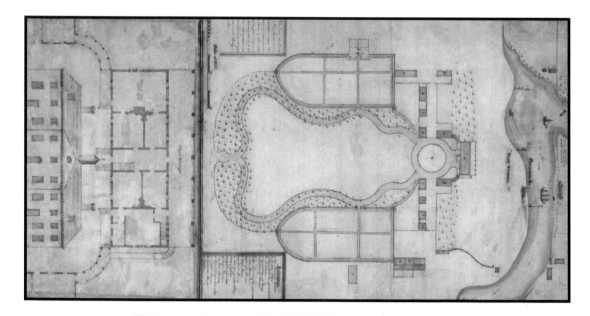

The ground plan of Washington's estate at Mount Vernon, drawn by Samuel Vaughan and presented to Washington in November 1787.

Washington's notes from his survey of a turnip field near Mount Vernon. Below left, a painting of his older brother, Lawrence Washington.

George joined the Virginia militia. In the militia he fought for the British, who ruled the American colonies. The militia battled the French for ownership of western lands in the French and Indian War.

In 1759, George married Martha Dandridge Custis, a widow with two young children named Jacky and Patsy.

---

## DID YOU KNOW?

Legend has it that George Washington had wooden teeth. Actually, he had dentures made of different materials, including hippopotamus ivory, cows' teeth, and metal.

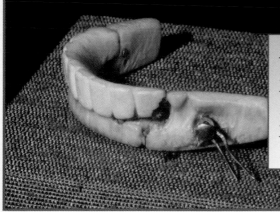

Above, a painting of the Washington family by Edward Savage. When Washington married Martha Custis, he adopted her two children. Left, Washington's false teeth, made of ivory.

The British government had many debts from its war with the French. To pay those debts, England imposed taxes on the American colonists. Many colonists believed it was unfair for England to tax them if they were not represented in the government. They were ready to fight for their independence.

When Britain imposed the Stamp Act, taxing all printed materials bearing a stamp, a Pennsylvania newspaper suggested that the stamp be a skull and crossbones.

Young Washington in the uniform of a colonial British colonel, the uniform he wore during the French and Indian War.

# 2   THE WAR
# FOR INDEPENDENCE

In September 1774, George Washington attended the First Continental Congress in Philadelphia as a representative from Virginia. Washington hoped to avoid war with England, but he did feel that the British government was unjust.

## A DIVIDED NATION

Only about a third of colonial Americans supported independence. A third were neutral, and another third were Tory, or pro-British.

The First Continental Congress, Philadelphia, 1774. The delegates debated whether to declare their independence from England.

13

On April 18, 1775, a group of British soldiers marched to Concord, Massachusetts, to seize the colonists' weapons. Paul Revere rode through the night, warning the colonists that the British were coming. At dawn on April 19, the first shot of the Revolutionary War was fired.

Paul Revere on his midnight ride. The Minutemen who responded were mostly farmers.

British troops march through the town of Concord, Massachusetts. They were defeated and driven back with heavy losses.

In June 1775, George Washington was appointed commander in chief of the American army. He thought that his troops could fight the British in large battles. But in the summer of 1776, the Americans were defeated at Brooklyn Heights in a big battle. Washington decided upon a strategy of raiding and guerrilla warfare.

Two wooden canteens of the type used by soldiers in the Continental army.

Washington and his troops retreat to Pennsylvania after their defeat at the Battle of Brooklyn.

On Christmas night, 1776, Washington and his troops crossed the Delaware River for a surprise attack on the British army the next day at Trenton, New Jersey. In one hour, the Americans captured almost 1,000 prisoners.

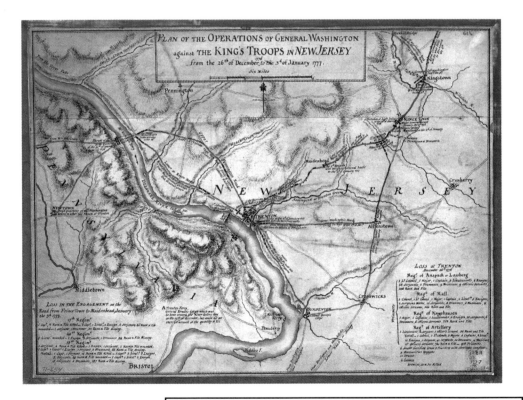

A map of the American attack on Trenton by the Continental army. There, Washington won an important victory.

Washington and his troops cross the Delaware River. From his base in Pennsylvania, Washington made bold raids into New Jersey, harassing the British troops.

After years of fighting, the Americans surrounded British forces at Yorktown, Virginia. Here the British surrendered to Washington in 1781. The Americans had won the Revolutionary War.

In May 1787, Washington attended the Constitutional Convention in Philadelphia. Out of this convention came the U.S. Constitution.

The Constitutional Convention in Philadelphia in 1787 drew up a new American constitution and created a strong federal government.

except what may be absolutely necessary for executing it *and inspection laws,* *and the net produce of all duties or imposts, laid by any State on imports, or exports, shall be for the use of the treasury of the United States: and all such laws shall be subject to revision & control of Congress*

No state shall, without the consent of Congress, lay imposts or duties on imports or exports, *with such consent, but to the use of the treasury of the United States* ~~and~~ keep troops nor ships

the same term, be elected ~~as follows~~

Each state shall appoint, in such manner as the legislature thereof may direct, a number of electors, equal to the whole number of senators and representatives to which the state may be entitled in Congress: but no senator or representative ~~shall~~ *nor any* person holding an office of trust or profit under the United States, *shall be appointed an Elector.* The electors shall meet in their respective states, and vote by ballot for two persons, of whom one at least shall not be an inhabitant of the same state with themselves. And they shall make a list of all the persons voted for, and of the number of votes for each; which list they shall sign and certify, and transmit sealed to the seat of the ~~general~~ government, directed to the president of the senate. The president of the senate shall in the presence of the senate and house of representatives open all the certificates, and the votes shall then be counted. The person having the greatest number of votes shall be the president, if such number be a majority of the whole number of electors appointed; and if there be more than one who have such majority, and have an equal number of votes, then the house of representatives shall immediately chuse by ballot one of them for president; and if no person have a majority, then from the five highest on the list the said house shall in like manner choose the president. But in choosing the president, the votes shall be taken by states ~~and not per capita~~, the representation from each state having one vote. A quorum for this purpose shall consist of a member or members from two-thirds of the states, and a majority of all the states shall be necessary to a choice. In every case, after the choice of the president ~~by the representatives~~, the person having the greatest number of votes of the electors shall be the vice-president. But if there should remain two or more who have equal votes, the senate shall choose from them by ballot the vice-president.

The Congress may determine the time of chusing the electors, and *the day on* which they shall give their votes; ~~which day~~ shall be ~~on~~ the same ~~day~~ throughout the United States.

No person except a natural born citizen, or a citizen of the United States, at the time of the adoption of this constitution, shall be eligible to the office of president; neither shall any person be eligible to that office who shall not have attained to the age of thirty-five years, and been fourteen years a resident within the United States.

In case of the removal of the president from office, or of his death, resignation, or inability to discharge the powers and duties of the said office, the same shall devolve on the vice-president, and the Congress may by law provide for the case of removal, death, resignation or inability, both of the president and vice-president, declaring what officer shall then act as president, and such officer shall act accordingly, until the disability be removed, or ~~a~~ president ~~shall~~ *shall be elected*

The president shall, at stated times, receive ~~for his services a compensation~~, which shall neither be encreased nor diminished during the period for which he shall have been elected. *and he shall not receive within that period any other emolument from the United States, or either of them.*

Before he enter on the execution of his office, he shall take the following oath or affirmation: "I——, do solemnly swear (or affirm) that I will faithfully execute the office of president of the United States, and will to the best of my ~~abilities~~, preserve, protect and defend the constitution of the United States."

Sect. 2. The president shall be commander in chief of the army and navy of the United States, *when called into the actual service of the United States* and of the militia of the several states; he may require the opinion, in writing, of the principal officer in each of the executive departments, upon any subject relating to the duties of their respective offices, ~~when called into the actual service of the United States~~, and he shall have power to grant reprieves and pardons for offences against the United States, except in cases of impeachment.

He shall have power, by and with the advice and consent of the senate, to make treaties, provided two-thirds of the senators present concur; and he shall nominate, and by and with the advice and consent of the senate, shall appoint ambassadors, other public ministers and consuls, judges of the supreme court, and all other officers of the United States, whose appointments are not herein otherwise provided for, *and which shall be established by law.*

The president shall have power to fill up all vacancies that may happen during the recess of the senate, by granting commissions which shall expire at the end of their next session. *But the Congress may by law vest the appointment of such inferior officers as they think proper, in the*

Sect. 3. He shall from time to time give to the Congress information of the state of the union, and recommend to their consideration such measures as he shall judge necessary and expedient: he may, on extraordinary occasions, convene both houses, or either of them, and in case of disagreement between them, with respect to the time of adjournment, he may adjourn them to such time as he shall think proper: he shall receive ambassadors and other public ministers; he shall take

# **3** PRESIDENT OF THE NEW NATION

When it was time to choose a president, George Washington was the first choice of the people. When the votes in the new electoral college were counted, Washington had received all of them. John Adams was elected vice president. George Washington was sworn in as the first president of the United States on April 30, 1789.

## A COMPROMISE WITH SLAVERY

Election of the president by electoral college was a political compromise so that states with large numbers of free citizens would not dominate the government.

Above, Federal Hall, the first seat of the government, in New York City. Below, a copy of Washington's inaugural address, the speech he gave upon accepting the presidency of the United States.

FEDERAL HALL.

*Ap 30 1789*

Fellow Citizens of the Senate
and
of the House of Representatives

Among the vicissitudes incident to life, no event could have filled me with greater anxieties than that of which the notification was transmitted by your order, and received on the 14th day of the present month. On the one hand, I was summoned by my Country, whose voice I can never hear but with veneration and love, from a retreat which I had cho-

One of President Washington's first tasks was to create departments within the government. Washington created the Departments of War, Treasury, and State. Henry Knox was made secretary of war. Alexander Hamilton became secretary of the treasury. Thomas Jefferson was appointed secretary of state.

A document written by Jefferson while he was secretary of state. His arguments with Hamilton caused Washington to hate political factions.

George Washington and his cabinet. Thomas Jefferson, secretary of state, is seated second from the right.

At the end of his term, Washington did not want to serve as president again. But when the votes were counted, he was elected again. In 1797, George Washington finally retired as president.

In his farewell address, Washington advised Americans to avoid permanent alliances and to avoid political factions at home.

## DEGREES AND HONORS

In his lifetime, George Washington received honorary degrees from Harvard, Yale, and Brown Universities. Today, these Ivy League schools are considered some of the best in America.

Friends, & Fellow-citizens

The period for a new election of a Citizen, to administer the Executive government of the United States, being not far distant, and the time actually arrived, when your thoughts must be employed in designating the person, who is to be cloathed with that important trust ~~for another~~ ~~term~~, it appears to me proper, especially as it may conduce to a more distinct expression of the public voice, that I should now apprise you of the resolution I have formed, to decline being considered among the number of those, out of whom a choice is to be made. —

I beg you, at the same time, to do me the justice to be assured that this resolution has not been taken, without a strict regard to all the considerations appertaining to the relation, which binds a dutiful citizen to his country — and that, in withdrawing the tender of service which silence

A copy of Washington's farewell address to the nation after serving two terms as president.

for your past kindness; but am supported by a full conviction

George was happy to go home to Mount Vernon. In December 1799, he caught a throat infection while riding his horse in the harsh winter weather. On December 14, 1799, he died at home in his bed. He was 67 years old.

A statue of George Washington on horseback stands atop a pedestal in the Public Garden next to Boston Common in Boston, Massachusetts.

An engraving of George Washington on his deathbed. In the eighteenth century, simple infections could be fatal.

G.WASHINGTON in his last Illness attended by Doctr Craik and Brown

# TIMELINE

1732—George Washington is born.

1748—Washington becomes a surveyor at age 16.

1759—Washington marries Martha Dandridge Custis.

1774—In September, Washington attends the First Continental Congress in Philadelphia as a representative of Virginia.

1775—On April 19, the first shot of the Revolutionary War is fired in Massachusetts; in June, Washington is appointed commander in chief of the Continental army.

1776—On July 4, Congress approves the Declaration of Independence; on Christmas night, Washington and his troops cross the Delaware River for a surprise attack on British troops.

1781—In October, the British surrender at Yorktown.

1783—In December, Washington retires from the military.

1789—On April 30, Washington is sworn in as the first president of the United States.

1797—Washington retires as president. Vice President John Adams is elected as the second president of the United States.

1799—In December, Washington catches a throat infection. He dies at the age of 67.

# GLOSSARY

**colony (KAH-luh-nee)** A settlement in a new country that is still controlled by another country.

**debt (DET)** Something owed.

**declaration (deh-kluh-RAY-shun)** A formal statement.

**militia (muh-LIH-shuh)** A group of citizens who are trained to fight but who only serve in a time of emergency.

**plantation (plan-TAY-shun)** A very large farm where crops are grown.

**representative (reh-prih-ZEN-tuh-tiv)** An elected spokesperson for a group of people.

**surrender (suh-REN-der)** To admit defeat to the enemy and lay down arms.

**taxes (TAKS-ez)** Money that the government takes from citizens to pay its expenses.

**widow (WIH-doh)** A woman whose husband has died.

## WEB SITES

Due to the changing nature of Internet links, the Rosen Publishing Group, Inc., has developed an online list of Web sites related to the subject of this book. This site is updated regularly. Please use this link to access the list:

http://www.rosenlinks.com/fpah/gwas

## PRIMARY SOURCE IMAGE LIST

**Page 5:** Plan of the City of Washington by Pierre Charles L'Enfant, Philadelphia, 1792, now with the Library of Congress. Portrait of George Washington by Gilbert Stuart, 1792, now with the National Portrait Gallery.

**Page 6:** Ground plan of Mount Vernon by Samuel Vaughan, 1787.

**Page 7:** From George Washington's second school copy book, 1747/1748, now with the Manuscript Division of the Library of Congress. Inset: Lawrence Washington, painted by John Wollaston in 1738, oil on canvas, courtesy of the Mount Vernon Ladies' Association.

**Page 9 (top):** *The Washington Family* by Edward Savage (1761–1796), oil on canvas, 1796, now with the National Gallery of Art.

**Page 10:** Woodcut from the *Pennsylvania Journal and Advertiser*.

**Page 11:** Portrait of George Washington as a colonial British officer, by Charles Wilson Peale, oil on canvas, 1772, now housed at Washington and Lee University, Lexington, Virginia.

**Page 13:** An engraving by Francois Godefoy of the First Continental Congress, Carpenter Hall, Philadephia, 1774.

**Page 14:** *Awaken . . .* by William Robinson Leigh, painted in 1917.

**Page 15:** *A View of the Town of Concord*, engraved in 1775 by Sidney L. Smith after a painting by Amos Doolittle, now housed at the New York Public Library.

**Page 19:** *Washington Crossing the Delaware* by Emanuel Gottlieb Leutze, 1851.
**Page 20:** The Constitutional Convention, Philadelphia, 1787.
**Page 21:** Draft of the Constitution with Washington's handwritten annotations, now with the Manuscript Division of the Library of Congress.
**Page 23 (bottom):** Handwritten draft of George Washington's first inaugural address, delivered to Congress at Federal Hall in New York City, 1789. Now with the Manuscript Division of the Library of Congress.
**Page 25:** Portrait of George Washington and his cabinet by Gilbert Stuart, 1805, now with the National Portrait Gallery.
**Page 27:** Final draft of George Washington's Farewell Address, 1796, now with the Library of Congress.
**Page 29:** George Washington in his last illness attended by Doctors Craik and Brown, by Currier and Ives, a hand-colored print, 1800, courtesy of the Mount Vernon Ladies' Association.

# INDEX

# ABOUT THE AUTHOR

Tracie Egan is a freelance writer who lives in New York City.